To: Cole & Cayleigh
From: Auntie Diane

Christmas 1998

Lots of love always!

Have You Seen Trees?

Have You Seen Trees?

BY JOANNE OPPENHEIM

ILLUSTRATED BY JEAN AND MOU-SIEN TSENG

SCHOLASTIC INC.

New York

Published by Scholastic Inc.
SCHOLASTIC HARDCOVER is a registered trademark
of Scholastic Inc.

Library of Congress Cataloging-in-Publication Data
Oppenheim, Joanne.
Have you seen trees? / by Joanne Oppenheim;
illustrated by Jean and Mou-sien Tseng.
p.   cm.
ISBN 0-590-46691-7
1. Trees—Juvenile literature. [1. Trees.] I. Tseng, Jean,
ill. II. Tseng, Mou-sien, ill. III. Title.
QK475.8.O67 1995
582.16 — dc20   94-14585
CIP
AC

12 11 10 9 8 7 6 5 4 3 2   5 6 7 8 9 0/09
Printed in Singapore   10

First printing, April 1995

Designed by Claire B. Counihan

The illustrations in this book were executed
with pen and watercolor on
gesso-primed paper.

To my grandson
Matthew Alexander —
welcome!
Love, J.O.

To our daughters
Grace and Ivy —
may your lives be
as colorful and fruitful
as the trees.
J. & M. T.

Have you seen trees?
High trees, wide trees,
reaching-to-the-sky trees.
Did you ever hide behind
a wide high tree?

Have you seen small trees?
Slow-to-grow, low trees?
I can touch the leaves
of the short small trees!

Have you seen fall trees?
Full, fall, nut trees —
walnut, chestnut,
butternut, hickorynut.
I like the taste
of the fall nut trees!

Red leaves, yellow leaves,
orange-falling-down leaves.
Have you seen the sight
of the bright fall leaves?

Dry leaves, brown leaves,
covering-the-ground leaves.
Make-a-crunching-sound leaves,
dropping-everywhere leaves,
left-the-trees-bare leaves.
I can hear the crunch
of the crisp dry leaves!

Cold tree, old tree,
planted-long-ago tree.
Holes in the bole
of a dark cold tree!

Wrinkled bark, rough bark,
twisted, corky, cracked bark.
White bark, smooth bark,
slick-without-a-groove bark.

Have you seen snow trees?
Winter, bright, white trees?
Turned-to-ice-at-night trees,
sparkling-in-the-light trees.
I can hear the SNAP
of the winter white trees!

What about winter green,
never bare evergreens?
Pineconed, white pine.
Prickly needled pitch pine.
I've seen pine of every kind.
Have you seen trees?

Have you seen spring trees?
Budding, bursting, blooming trees!
Yellow, pink, and green trees!
Sticky, dripping sap trees,
dropping seeds and popping leaves.
Singing birds in nesting trees.
Bugs in the bark of the
spring green trees!

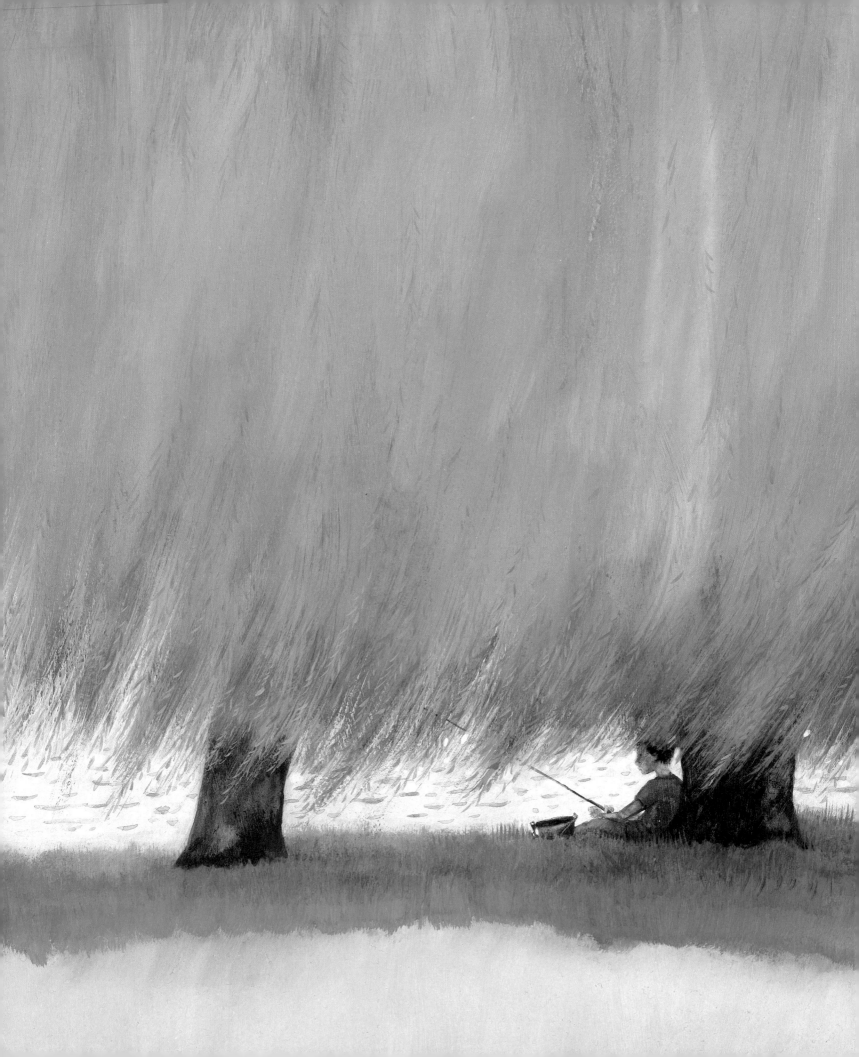

Have you seen summer trees?
Shade-me-from-the-light trees.

Whisper-in-the-night trees.
I can hear the trees!

No dogs
in the dogwood.
Nor cotton
in the cottonwood.
No iron
in the ironwood.
Nor buttons
in the buttonwood.
Just good wood!

Nannyberry, mulberry,
hackberry, sheepberry.
Birds in the berries
of a sassafras tree.
Wild cherry, chokecherry,
every kind of cherry berry!

Peach tree,
pear tree,
an orchard full
of apple trees.

A million trees, a billion leaves,
a forest with a zillion trees.

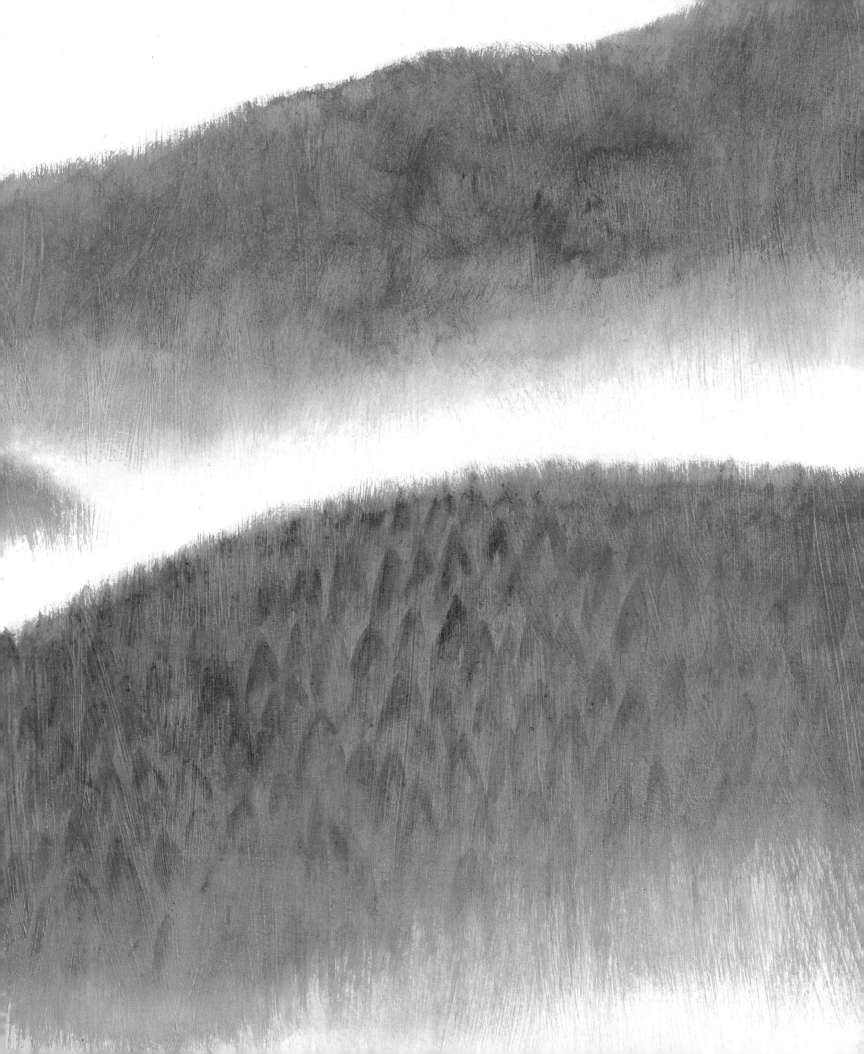

Have you seen trees?

Have you seen *these* trees?

ASH
The wood from ash trees is used to make baseball bats, hockey sticks, and tennis rackets.

CEDAR
The scent of cedar wood keeps moths away. This is why clothing is often stored with cedar blocks.

CHESTNUT
Many people feel that the tastiest nuts come from the chestnut tree.

CRAB APPLE
Crab apples are used to make jellies and ciders.

FIR

Fir trees make good Christmas trees because their needles don't fall off quickly.

GINGKO

The gingko tree existed during the time of the dinosaurs. You might call it a living fossil!

OAK

An acorn is the seed of an oak tree. Squirrels eat acorns but the ones they bury and forget may grow into new oak trees.

PALM

The double coconut is the fruit of a palm tree. It is the biggest seed in the world.

REDWOOD

Redwood trees number among the tallest trees. They can grow from 200 to 300 feet tall and from 20 to 30 feet across the center of the tree.

SASSAFRAS

Parts of the sassafras tree can be used to make two different drinks: tea and root beer.

SHAGBARK HICKORY

The trunk of the shagbark hickory tree looks like strips of shredded bark, hence the tree's "shaggy" appearance — and its name.

SPRUCE

The wood of the spruce tree is used for making paper and stringed instruments like the violin.

SUGAR MAPLE

The sap from the sugar maple tree is used to make syrup. It takes 30 gallons of maple sap to make one gallon of syrup.

SWEET GUM

The sap of a sweet gum tree is used to make perfumes and medicines. It can also be chewed like bubble gum.

UMBRELLA

The needles of the umbrella tree look like the spokes of an umbrella. The wood of the umbrella tree is good for making boats.

WEEPING WILLOW

The bark of some willow trees contains an acid that is similar to quinine, the main ingredient in aspirin.